The Illustrators of Alice

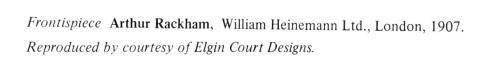

THE ILLUSTRATORS OF
ALICE IN WONDERLAND
AND
THROUGH THE LOOKING GLASS

edited by

Graham Ovenden

with an introduction by

John Davis

ACADEMY EDITIONS   LONDON

ST. MARTIN'S PRESS   NEW YORK

We would like to thank the many publishers who have given us permission to reproduce illustrations from their editions; and June Moll of the University of Texas, Stanley Marx, Peter Blake and Dr. Selwyn Goodacre for their assistance in compiling the list of illustrators and providing information on books in their collections. Also to Leslie Waddington for his help in lending material for colour reproduction.

First published in 1972 in Great Britain by
Academy Editions, 7 Holland Street, London W.8.
Published in the United States of America by
St. Martin's Press, New York, N.Y. 10010.

Designed by Prangtong Jitasiri.

Library of Congress Catalog No. 72 - 76911.

Printed and bound in Great Britain by The Pitman Press, Bath.

Introduction
by

John Davis

Well over a hundred artists have illustrated Lewis Carroll's *Alice's Adventures in Wonderland* and *Through the Looking-Glass and What Alice Found There* since they were first published in 1865 and 1871. Clearly these books have fascinated artists in the same way as they have appealed to readers. The treatment of Carroll's characters has varied from the surrealistic to the mundane: contemporary events and attitudes are frequently reflected — the cost of the Mad Hatter's hat fluctuating with current prices, the Playing Cards wearing Prussian helmets, in pre-1914 illustrations, demarcation-conscious Trade Unionists disputing over the painted rose tree. But in outlining the approach that a number of artists have taken, any order of merit is purely subjective. From the many illustrations reproduced, the reader can make his own judgement.

To discuss Alice's illustrations without discussing Alice's creator would be impossible. Charles Lutwidge Dodgson, the son of the Rector of Daresbury in Cheshire, was born on January 17th, 1832. He was educated at Richmond, Yorkshire, and Rugby and in 1851 came into residence at Christ Church, Oxford, with which he was to be associated for the rest of his life; inevitably college life and politics are closely woven into much of his writing. In 1854 he graduated and in 1855 was appointed Sub-Librarian of Christ Church. By the end of the year he became in his own words 'master and tutor in Ch.Ch., with an income of more than £300 a year and the course of mathematical tuition marked out by God's providence for at least some years to come.' He was ordained deacon in 1861 but never proceeded to priest's orders.

From 1845 onwards Charles Dodgson wrote prose and poems for a number of public and private magazines and in 1856 Lewis Carroll was born, although, at the time, nobody recognized him. In that year, when writing for *The Train*, he felt the need of a pseudonym and proposed a number of alternatives to the magazine's editor, Edmund Yates. The first suggested names were typical of his mental processes — Edgar Cuthwellis or Edgar U.C. Westhall, anagrams of his christian names Charles Lutwidge. The second two proposals were Louis Carroll or Lewis Carroll, variants of Charles, Carolus, Carroll and Lutwidge, Ludovicus, Lewis. Edmund Yates chose Lewis Carroll and from the publication of the poem *Solitude* in March 1856, this became Dodgson's *nom de plume* for his non-academic publications, Dodgson being retained for his mathematical writings.

Lewis Carroll, 1886.

Willy Pogany, 1929.

A.L. Bowley, 1921.

On July 4th, 1862 there was a very important entry in Carroll's diary, 'I made an expedition up the river to Godstow with the three Liddells; we had tea on the bank there, and did not reach Christ Church again till half past eight.' This short sentence describes the first telling of *Alice's Adventures in Wonderland* to Alice, Lorina and Edith Liddell, the three daughters of Dean Liddell of Christ Church. On Carroll's return to Oxford that evening he promised to write out his story but it was some time before that promise was fulfilled. By January 1863 the manuscript was completed and illustrated with some of Carroll's pen and ink sketches; and was shown to Henry Kingsley, the writer of *The Water Babies*, who urged Carroll to publish it since he immediately recognised its merit. Other friends including Duckworth and George Macdonald were approached for comments and again enthusiastic responses were received. Over the next one and a half years Carroll rewrote his story but realising his lack of skill as an artist, he looked about for a professional illustrator. In February 1864, following an introduction from Tom Taylor, he approached John Tenniel who had already illustrated several children's books including *Undine* and *Aesop's Fables*. Tenniel seems to have taken some months to consider the proposal but final agreement was reached in April.

Charles Robinson, 1907.

Tenniel was a mild and gentle man but his relationship with Carroll was stormy though mutually concealed beneath a veneer of Victorian politeness. Carroll is said to have told Harry Furniss that he had not liked any of Tenniel's drawings except Humpty Dumpty! The original child of Carroll's story was Alice Liddell but Tenniel's illustrations were undoubtedly based on Mary Hilton Badcock (p.102) a photograph of whom Carroll sent to Tenniel with the suggestion that she might make a good model; Tenniel probably worked straight from the photograph as he rarely used live models. Tenniel's illustrations for *Alice's Adventures in Wonderland* are a perfect example of the combination between artist and author and to many they are inseparable. Perhaps Tenniel's weakness, if any be admitted, is in his drawings of Alice herself who frequently appears overly serious and expressionless (pp. 40, 58). But he must be placed unequivocally as one if not the greatest of the many illustrators of Alice.

Gwynedd Hudson, 1922.

When Tenniel had finished the drawings, Carroll persuaded Macmillan, publishers to Oxford University to undertake publication of *Alice's Adventures in Wonderland* on a common basis. In July 1865 the first edition was issued. Two weeks after publication, Tenniel told Carroll that he was dissatisfied with the reproduction of the illustrations and Carroll called in as many as he could of the fifty or so copies that had been given away to his child friends or that had been sold. A second edition, the type reset and printed by Richard Clay, was published in November 1865 but dated 1866. The unbound sheets of the first edition were not

Philip Gough, c. 1940.

scrapped but sold to America where they were bound up with a new frontispiece and issued in 1866.

Carroll was now achieving international fame from his book and translations, with the Tenniel illustrations, appeared in French, German and Italian, whilst several editions were published in the U.S.A. Within a year, he had decided upon a sequel but determined to find a suitable artist first. His initial approach to Tenniel, who had found Carroll very fussy to work with, was rejected. Carroll then approached a number of other artists, including Richard Doyle and Sir Noel Paton, even considering W.S.Gilbert, but all politely refused. Tenniel eventually accepted only after Carroll's renewed pleading. The successful team was thus reunited to quarrel and bicker once more but, perhaps, in *Through the Looking-Glass,* to present a more impressive and a more united book.

Tenniel's reputation had also been enhanced by his *Wonderland* illustrations, and he appears to have taken a stronger and even more forceful line with this second book. Carroll continued to maintain his independence advising. 'Don't give Alice so much crinoline' and 'The White Knight must not have whiskers;' but Tenniel's knight was whiskered and old and, reputedly, bore a striking resemblance to one of his colleagues in *Punch,* a certain Ponny Mayhew. Tenniel also managed to convince Carroll to shorten his book from thirteen chapters to twelve following correspondence containing such remarks as 'Don't think me brutal, but I am bound to say that the '*wasp*' chapter doesn't interest me in the least and I can't see my way to a picture. If you want to shorten the book, I can't help thinking-with all submission-that here is your opportunity.' He also remarked that a 'wasp in a wig is beyond the appliance of art.' *Through the Looking-Glass* and *What Alice Found There* was published in time for Christmas 1871, though the first edition was dated 1872; it was an immediate success and like his *Wonderland* has been reprinted many times.

Once again Tenniel had excelled himself with fifty illustrations compared with the forty-two in *Wonderland.* Again his mastery of animals and humans was apparent and in this book, his drawings of Alice seem softer and less wooden; his interpretation and technique both superb, his Jabberwocky is suitably fearsome whilst the original frontispiece of the White Knight seems to have an echo of Durer in both composition and print quality. It is interesting, too, that the pictures of Alice entering and emerging from the looking-glass (p. 98) appear on subsequent pages, as if her entry into wonderland was happening in the book, itself. The combination of artist and writer seems more satisfying in this, than in the preceding work, and is perhaps best described in the words of one of Tenniel's biographers who said that there may be better drawings but no better illustrations.

'Alice took up the fan and gloves, and, as the hall was very hot, she kept fanning herself all the time she went on talking!

Mabel Lucie Attwell, 1910.

Before examining the rest of Alice's illustrators, the one to be considered is Lewis Carroll himself. Indeed he should be regarded as the first illustrator of *Alice in Wonderland* as his original manuscript for Alice Liddell included many of his own sketches. However, his confidence in his own artistic ability must have been sapped when Ruskin remarked that he had not enough talent to make it worth his while to devote much time to sketching. Carroll did not possess the technical expertise of Tenniel but he did try to represent the characters that he had created. As the central character Alice appears in twenty-seven of the thirty-seven illustrations whilst Tenniel only pictured her twenty-three times in his forty-two pictures. Carroll's Alice is a serious-minded little girl quite capable of coping with the illogical wonderland. It is understandable that these drawings lacked appeal to the upper middle class children's readership of the nineteenth century whose taste was largely dictated by their parents. However, Carroll's drawings warrant reassessment now that technical accuracy in presentation is no longer held in such high esteem. In their way they have a soul which is lacking in those of Tenniel and are much more moving. Carroll arranged for the text and pictures to be published in 1886 under the title of *Alice's Adventures Under Ground.* This was not a success and only one edition was printed in Carroll's lifetime.

Mervyn Peake, 1954.

Whilst Carroll was alive, few artists had either the wish or the opportunity to compete with Tenniel's illustrations. In 1884, Stanley Leathes produced *Alice's Wonderland Birthday Book* which contained a number of illustrations by J.P.M. (p.50). There is a Carroll quotation for each day, facing pages arranged for birthday entries. The book was produced with Carroll's full permission and is unusual mainly because he allowed an artist other than Tenniel to illustrate his stories. The pictures themselves are undoubtedly based on those of Tenniel but are sufficiently different to be of interest. In 1896, some two years before Carroll's death in 1898, Blanche McManus illustrated an American edition of *Alice in Wonderland*. There seems to be no record of any comments by Carroll on these drawings which are pleasant but undistinguished.

The flood of illustrated editions of *Alice in Wonderland* started shortly after Carroll's death. First in the United States, then in Britain. Between 1899 and 1904 four further American editions were published of which the best-known was that of Peter Newell. Newell produced forty pictures for an elegantly designed edition, the text surrounded with beautiful ornamental designs, but the drawings having a flat theatrical quality with neither the simplicity to endear them to children nor the perception to appeal to adults and in no way rivalling the humour and the draughtsmanship of Tenniel. In 1907 the British copyright in *Alice in Wonderland* expired and there was an almost indecent rush by

Sir John Tenniel, 1872.

publishers to produce editions with new illustrations; at least eight being published in the autumn of that year.

The first, issued in October, was the Chatto and Windus edition with coloured drawings by Millicent Sowerby. Despite an unusual title page, (p.15) the pictures are uninspired, though pleasing, and the whole production disappointing considering that one had been waiting for forty years for a successor to Tenniel.

The next edition, published towards the end of 1907, was illustrated by Thomas Maybank, and memorable more for its production so soon after the expiration of the copyright than for an individual pictorial interpretation of the text, (pp. 39, 62). This was followed by that of Arthur Rackham, already well known as an illustrator of children's books before he tackled Alice and he must be regarded as the first artist to bear comparison to Tenniel. His water colours are magnificent with a haunting quality (p.4); browns and greys predominating in his compositions, he excels in his backgrounds of gnarled trees with mischievous eyes, which occasionally dominate the characters. His Alice (p.33) is maturer than Tenniel's, whilst his Mad Hatter has a sharper East End quality and, in fact, has reduced the price of his hat from 10/6 to 8/11.

Also in November, 1907, came an edition with eight coloured plates and one hundred and twelve other illustrations by Charles Robinson. The Robinson brothers were talented artists, Charles and Thomas Heath both illustrated *Alice in Wonderland,* although the task was not undertaken by their more famous brother William Heath, the humorous contributor to *Punch.* Charles's illustrations are quite delightful and amongst the many there must be some to suit all tastes. His picture of Alice creating the Pool of Tears (p.21), thoroughly captures the particular passage in the text, whilst that of the Frog Footman (p.38) or the Gryphon (p.56) are typical of the individual sketches scattered throughout the book. Scarcely a page passes without an illustration which is, after all, how a children's book should be presented, particularly in 1907. Charles Robinson's pictures are memorable and it seems a pity that this edition does not seem to have been reprinted since 1928.

Of the eight illustrated editions of *Alice in Wonderland* issued in 1907, those by Arthur Rackham and Charles Robinson appear to be the only two which captured the story in a new but memorable style. Alice Ross's pictures are slight and clearly based on Tenniel; W.H.Walker draws a graceful Alice, particularly as she rises out of the Pool of Tears (p.20) and his Mad Hatter has slashed the price to 3/6 for a curious bowler hat (p.37). His are a straightforward, competent set of illustrations, blending well with the story.

Charles Robinson, 1907.

Sir John Tenniel, 1866.

A.E. Jackson, 1915.

From 1908 onwards new illustrators tackled *Alice in Wonderland* almost every year. Each obviously contributed his own style and expertise but few produced a really original approach and many seemed prosaic in performance as if under instructions from their publisher to illustrate Lewis Carroll's book after *Robinson Crusoe* and before *Grimm's Fairy Tales.* The New Zealander Harry Rountree (1908) was another of the *Punch* artists to tackle Alice. His animals are good though perhaps a little fussy, but the human characters lack conviction. A.E. Jackson (1915) produced a series of pleasantly coloured illustrations with a more contemporary Alice, a splendid Mad Hatter and a beautifully coiffeured un-ugly Duchess.

Charles Robinson's brother Thomas Heath Robinson jointly illustrated *Alice in Wonderland* with Charles Pears. This is interesting as it is rare for two artists to undertake such a task and to be honest there seems to have been little if any collaboration between the two illustrators: Alice, the Mad Hatter and the March Hare are each interpreted in completely different ways. Pears merely redraws Tenniel's pictures in colour whilst Thomas Heath produces a set of charming illustrations. His interpretation of the meeting between Alice, who throughout these pictures is more mature than is customary, and the Pigeon is exquisite (p.32). One wonders at the reason for this joint production as alone Thomas Heath Robinson could have created a book comparable to but different from that of his brother Charles.

Harry Furniss, 1926.

One artist stands out during the rather barren wilderness of the twenties and thirties, Willy Pogany (1929). His Art Deco illustrations have an altogether new, crisp, clean style — the first really original interpretation since Tenniel — and are a milestone in the artistic characterization of Alice. Alice is a 30's American bobbysoxer with a page boy hair style and the Mad Hatter (p.37) is definitely a member of the rag trade; of the playing cards, the clubs appear as West Point cadets, the diamonds and hearts straight from the Ziegfield Follies Chorus line (p.48) whilst the spades are obviously members of the painters' and decorators' union. D.R. Sexton (1933) also produced a 30's Alice with lipstick and eye shadow (p.31) but sadly lacking the depth of Pogany's re-interpretation.

Of contemporary artists who have illustrated *Wonderland* Ralph Steadman (1967) has produced a series of pictures in a style probably appealing only to adults, totally different from that of any predecessor. His comparisons between Carroll characters and present day equivalents is astute and although his drawings may not attract all Alice lovers, he must be recognized as the first artist to attempt a radical re-interpretation. Salvador Dali's series of lithographs for a magnificent limited edition (1969), which unfortunately proved technically impossible to reproduce in this selection.

Sir John Tenniel, 1866.

are pure surrealism. Alice, with a skipping rope, recurs in all the drawings; the table top upon which the Mad Hatter's tea party is held is formed from one of Dali's melting watches, and, in another picture, Alice's hand protrudes from a typical Mediterranean villa. Max Ernst (1970) illustrated the Mad Hatter's tea party in *Lewis Carroll's Wonderland,* a selection of Carroll's logic and letters, in a lithograph where words are compressed in a mathematical pattern (p. 54) Graham Ovenden whose complete Alice paintings and screen-prints have not yet been published in book form, has taken a unique and personal approach: in all his illustrations, only Alice is depicted. In every case, her reaction to a particular situation is emphasized. Drawn with immense sensitivity and depth of feeling for Carroll's story, they have a timeless quality that must appeal even to the purists amongst Alice lovers.

Margaret Tarrant, 1916.

Alice in Wonderland has surely been illustrated by more artists than any other children's book; one is tempted to say than any other fictional work. But *Through the Looking Glass* does not seem to have had the same appeal. Several artists have illustrated both volumes, only a mere four seem to have tackled *Looking-Glass* alone: Franklin Hughes, Nan Fullerton, Bridgeman and Peter Blake. The majority of publishers seem to have been content to reprint Tenniel's illustrations.

The first British edition with new illustrations, by Harry Rountree, was published in 1928. Again, his animal characters are the best feature. But in the United States there were several earlier editions. Blanche McManus (1899) was again the first with a set of illustrations that repeat the limitations of those she designed for *Wonderland* (pp.83,90). Peter Newell's *Through the Looking-Glass* (1901) is more successful, the pictures more in tune with the text than those he did for *Wonderland,* but the round faced oriental chess pieces pall (pp.77,94) and the glossy photographic re-productions of his drawings become tedious. It was not until the thirties onwards, both in England and America, that some really distinguished illustrations were produced.

Robert Högfeldt, 1945.

Of these a set of elegant watercolours by the American artist Franklin Hughes (1931) combine the rather flat geometric style of much of American art of the 30's with a curiously contemporary quality (p.76). In England, Edgar Thurstan produced a striking set of pictures at about the same time. His Alice is more mature than in many other portrayals, although not as surprisingly adult as J.Morton Sale's (p.84), and his Humpty Dumpty reminds one of an insecure business executive just about to fall off his chair (p.87). Indeed, in both this and the next decade some of the most interesting editions were published. Philip Gough set both books in a delightful rococo background, his Tweedledum and Tweedle-dee depicted as minor French courtiers (p.80); the Scandin-

Arthur Rackham, 1907.

avian Robert Högfeldt (1945), one of the few foreign artists whose pictures were published in an English-language edition produced a series of splendid animals – particularly the Mock Turtle whose sadness pervades the page.

But perhaps the most memorable interpretation comes from Mervyn Peake (1954) of whose illustrations Graham Greene wrote 'You are the first person who has been able to illustrate the book satisfactorily since Tenniel, though I still argue as I think I argued with you years ago that your Alice is a little bit too much of a gamin,' This gamin quality of Alice is set against the weird, almost macabre, drawings of the other characters such as the Mad Hatter (p.43). In common with several artists who illustrated both books, Peake's drawings are even more successful in *Through the Looking-Glass* than *Wonderland* (p.89). Recently Peter Blake (1970) has produced a set of water-colours. He has totally immersed himself in *Through the Looking-Glass* and the series is superb. This edition has not yet been published, but at long last an artist rather than an illustrator has been inspired by this book and the result is worth waiting for.

Inevitably, Tenniel's illustrations have deeply influenced the work of nearly all the other artists who have approached *Alice in Wonderland* and *Through the Looking-Glass*; this is understandable as the various characters are meticulously described by Carroll who left little scope for the artist to do much more than embellish the story. This introduction has only sketched out the history of the writing and publication of the two books and summarized the work of certain artists. A detailed analysis would need a much lengthier study but for those interested in further reading on the subject, a short bibliography of works on Carroll (p.101) and one of illustrated English language editions has been included (p.99).

It would be naive to regard this list as comprehensive but it is more complete than any previously published. It does not include the names of artists who have modestly said that their pictures are 'after Tenniel', nor has an attempt been made to list artists who have illustrated foreign language editions, although some pictures from such editions have been selected.

Have any artists succeeded in meeting the challenge of Tenniel? Pride of place amongst other illustrators must go to Lewis Carroll himself, Rackham, Pogany, Peake, Steadman, Dali, Ernst, Blake and Ovenden, but another lover of the Alice books could and probably would create a totally different list.

'First she tried to look down and make out what she was coming to but it was too dark to see anything; then she looked at the sides of the well and noticed that they were filled with cupboards and book-shelves; here and there she saw maps and pictures hung upon pegs.'

Willy Pogany, 1929.

ALICE'S ADVENTURES
IN WONDERLAND

BY
LEWIS
CARROLL

Millicent Sowerby. Title page from the Chatto & Windus edition, London, 1907.

Chapter 1

DOWN THE RABBIT-HOLE

'but when the Rabbit actually *took a watch out of its waistcoat-pocket*, and looked at it, and then hurried on, Alice started to her feet.'

A.L. Bowley. Raphael Tuck & Sons Ltd., London, 1921.

H.N. Monro. *Children's Treasury of Great Stories,* Daily Express Publications, London, 1933.

Chapter 2

THE POOL OF TEARS

'Poor Alice! It was as much as she could do, lying down on one side, to look through into the garden with one eye: but to get through was more hopeless than ever: she sat down and began to cry again.'

Thomas Maybank, G. Routledge & Sons Ltd., London, 1907.

'Alice felt so desperate that she was ready to ask help of any one; so, when the Rabbit came near her, she began, in a low, timid voice, "If you please, Sir – " The Rabbit started violently, dropped the white kid gloves and fan, and scurried away into the darkness as hard as he could go.'

Thomas Heath Robinson, William Collins, London, 1922.

'The Rabbit started violently, dropped the white kid gloves and the fan, and scurried away into the darkness as hard as he could go.'

Sir John Tenniel, Macmillan, London, 1866.

'It was high time to go, for the pool was getting quite crowded with the birds and animals that had fallen into it: there was a Duck and a Dodo, a Lory and an Eaglet, and several other curious creatures. Alice led the way and the whole party swam to the shore.'

W.H. Walker. John Lane, The Bodley Head, London, 1907.

' "You ought to be ashamed of yourself," said Alice, "a great girl like you" (she might well say this), "to go on crying in this way! Stop this moment, I tell you!" But she went on all the same, shedding gallons of tears, until there was a large pool all around her.'

Charles Robinson. Cassell & Co. Ltd., London, 1907.

Chapter 3

A Caucus-race and a Long Tale

Philip Gough. The Heirloom Press, c. 1940.

Sir John Tenniel. Macmillan, London, 1866.

'At last the Mouse, who seemed to be a person of some authority among them, called out "Sit down all of you, and listen to me! *I'll* soon make you dry enough!" They all sat down at once in a large ring, with the Mouse in the middle. Alice kept her eyes anxiously fixed on it, for she felt sure she would catch a bad cold if she did not get very dry soon.'

" 'William the Conqueror, whose cause was favoured by the Pope, was soon submitted to by the English, who wanted leaders, and had been of late much accustomed to usurption and conquest. Edwin and Morcar, the Earls of Mercia and Northumbria . . . declared for him.' "

Franz Haacken. Georg Bitter Verlag, Berlin, 1970.

Chapter 4

The Rabbit sends in a Little Bill

Rene Cloke. Peter Gawthorne, London, 1944.

Sir John Tenniel. Macmillan, London, 1866.

'Still she went on growing, and, as a last resource she put one arm out of the window, and one foot up the chimney, and said to herself: "Now I can do no more, whatever happens. What will become of me?" '

'She went on growing and growing, and very soon had to kneel down on the floor: in another minute there was not even room for this, and she tried the effect of lying down with one elbow against the door, and the other arm curled round her head.'

Lewis Carroll. *Alice's Adventures Under Ground*, Macmillan, London, 1886.

' "And yet what a dear little puppy it was!" said Alice, as she leant against a buttercup to rest herself, and fanned herself with one of the leaves.'

J. Morton Sale, William Clowes, London, 1933.

B.P. Gutmann, 1920.

' "That you wo'n't!" thought Alice, and after waiting till she fancied she heard the Rabbit just under the window, she suddenly spread out her hand, and made a snatch in the air. She did not get hold of anything, but she heard a little shriek and a fall, and a crash of broken glass . . .'

Charles Robinson. Cassell & Co. Ltd., London, 1907.

26

Chapter 5

Advice from a Caterpillar

' "three inches is such a wretched height to be." "It is a very good height indeed!" said the Caterpillar angrily, rearing itself upright as it spoke (it was exactly three inches high).'

Harry Rountree.   The Children's Press, London, undated.

Photoplay. Non-Pareil Feature Film Corporation, Grosset & Dunlap, New York, c. 1915.

'The Caterpillar and Alice looked at each other for some time in silence: at last the Caterpillar took the hookah out of its mouth, and addressed her in a languid, sleepy voice.'

Sir John Tenniel. Macmillan, London, 1866.

"You are old, Father William," the young man said
    "And your hair has become very white;
And yet you incessantly stand on your head -
    Do you think, at your age, it is right?"

"In my youth," Father William replied to his son,
    "I feared it might injure the brain;
But, now that I'm perfectly sure I have none,
    Why, I do it again and again."

"You are old," said the youth, "as I mentioned before,
    And have grown most uncommonly fat;
Yet you turned a back-somersault in at the door -
    Pray, what is the reason of that?"

"In my youth," said the sage, as he shook his grey locks
    "I kept all my limbs very supple
By the use of this ointment - one shilling the box -
    Allow me to sell you a couple?"

Philip Gough, The Heirloom Press, c. 1940.

30

' "And now which is which?" she said to herself, and nibbled a little of the right-hand bit to try the effect: the next moment she felt a violent blow underneath her chin; it had struck her foot!'

D.R. Sexton. Juvenile Productions Ltd., London, 1933.

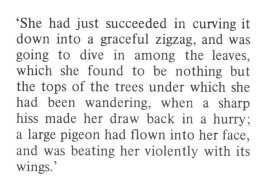

Millicent Sowerby. Chatto & Windus, London, 1907.

'She had just succeeded in curving it down into a graceful zigzag, and was going to dive in among the leaves, which she found to be nothing but the tops of the trees under which she had been wandering, when a sharp hiss made her draw back in a hurry; a large pigeon had flown into her face, and was beating her violently with its wings.'

' "Come, my head's free at last!" said Alice in a tone of delight, which changed into alarm in another moment, when she found that her shoulders were nowhere to be found; all she could see, when she looked down, was an immense length of neck, which seemed to rise like a stalk out of a sea of green leaves that lay far below her.'

Thomas Heath Robinson. William Collins, London, 1922.

' "Serpent!" screamed the Pigeon. "I'm not a serpent!" said Alice indignantly.
"Let me alone!" '

Arthur Rackham. William Heinemann, London, 1907

Charles Robinson, Cassell & Co., London, 1907.

Lewis Carroll. *Alice's Adventures Under Ground.* Macmillan, London, 1866.

'Just as she said this, she noticed that one of the trees had a door leading right into it. "That's very curious!" she thought. "But everything's curious today. I think I may as well go in at once." And in she went.'

Alice in Wonderland, Chapter VII

'It was the White Rabbit returning, splendidly dressed, with a pair of white kid gloves in one hand and a large fan in the other:'

Eleonora Mann. Jan Leendertz & Zoon, Amsterdam, c.1890.

Willy Pogany, 1929.

Harry Furniss, 1926.

A.L. Bowley, 1921.

Thomas Maybank, 1907.

W.H. Walker, 1907.

Willy Pogany. ' "The Dormouse is asleep again," said the Hatter, and he poured a little hot tea upon its nose.'

A.L. Bowley, Harry Furniss. ' "We quarrelled last March - just before *he* went mad, you know -" (pointing with his teaspoon at the March Hare,) "- it was at the great concert given by the Queen of Hearts, and I had to sing *'Twinkle, twinkle, little bat!'* "'

Thomas Maybank. 'The first witness was the Hatter. He came in with a teacup in one hand and a piece of bread-and-butter in the other!'

W.H. Walker. ' "You may go " said the King, and the Hatter hurriedly left the court'

(top left) **Rene Cloke.** Peter Gawthorne, London, 1944.
(bottom left) **A.E. Jackson.** Henry Frowde:Hodder & Stoughton, London, 1915.

Chapter 6

Pig and Pepper

'the First Footman was gone, and the other was sitting on the ground near the door, staring stupidly up into the sky.'

Charles Robinson. Cassell & Co. Ltd., London, 1907.

' "Oh, there's no use in talking to him," said Alice desperately: "He is perfectly idiotic!" And she opened the door and went in.'

Helen Monro. *Children's Treasury of Great Stories,* Daily Express, London, 1933.

' "I shall sit here," the Footman remarked, "till to-morrow — " At this moment the door of the house opened, and a large plate came skimming out, straight at the Footman's head: it just grazed his nose, and broke to pieces against one of the trees behind him. " — or next day, maybe," he continued in the same tone, exactly as if nothing had happened.'

Thomas Maybank. G. Routledge & Sons, Ltd., London, 1907.

'As soon as she had made out the proper way of nursing it (which was to twist it up into a sort of knot, and then keep tight hold of its right ear and left foot, so as to prevent its undoing itself), she carried it out into the open air.'

Robert Högfeldt. Jan Forlag, Stockholm, 1945.

' "If you're going to turn into a pig, my dear," said Alice, seriously, "I'll have nothing to do with you. Mind now!" The poor little thing sobbed again (or grunted, it was impossible to say which), and they went on for some while in silence.'

Sir John Tenniel. Macmillan, London, 1866.

Willy Pogany

'The door led right into a large kitchen, which was full of smoke from one end to the other : the Duchess was sitting on a three-legged stool in the middle, nursing a baby: the cook was leaning over the fire, stirring a large cauldron which seemed to be full of soup. "There's certainly too much pepper in that soup!" Alice said to herself, as well as she could for sneezing. There was certainly too much of it in the *air*. Even the Duchess sneezed occasionally; and as for the baby, it was sneezing and howling alternately without a moment's pause. The only two creatures in the kitchen that did *not* sneeze, were the cook, and a large cat, which was lying on the hearth and grinning from ear to ear.'

Willy Pogany. E.P. Dutton & Co., New York, 1929.

Chapter 7

A MAD TEA-PARTY

B.P. Gutmann,   George G. Harrap, London, 1920.

Sir John Tenniel.   Macmillan, London, 1866.

Mervyn Peake, Allen Wingate, London, 1954.

'This piece of rudeness was more than Alice could bear: she got up in great disgust, and walked off:' the Dormouse fell asleep instantly, and neither of the others took the least notice of her going, though she looked back once or twice, half hoping that they would call after her: the last time she saw them, they were trying to put the Dormouse into the teapot. "At any rate I'll never go *there* again!" said Alice, as she picked her way through the wood.'

Harry Rountree. The Children's Press, London, undated.

K.M.R. S.W. Partridge & Co., London, 1908.

'The table was a large one, but the three were all crowded together at one corner of it. "No room! No room!" they cried out when they saw Alice coming. "There's plenty of room!" said Alice indignantly, and she sat down in a large arm-chair at one end of the table.'

Willy Pogany. E.P. Dutton & Co., New York, 1929.

'This piece of rudeness was more than Alice could bear: she got up in great disgust, and walked off: the Dormouse fell asleep instantly, and neither of the others took the least notice of her going, though she looked back once or twice, half hoping that they would call after her.'

Graham Ovenden, pencil, 1969.

Chapter 8

THE QUEEN'S CROQUET-GROUND

Lewis Carroll, 1886.

Sir John Tenniel, 1866.

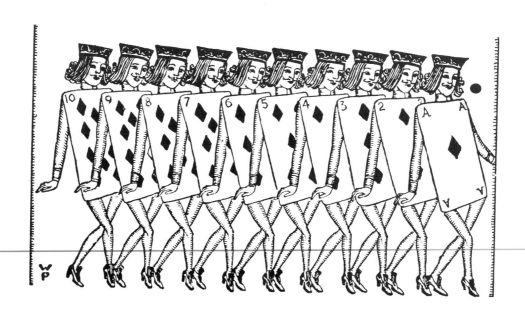

'First came ten soldiers carrying clubs, . . . next the ten courtiers; these were ornamented all over with diamonds, and walked two and two, as the soldiers did.'

Willy Pogany, E.P. Dutton & Co. Ltd., New York, 1929.

48

' "Look out now, Five! Don't go splashing paint over me like that!" "I couldn't help it," said Five, in a sulky tone. "Seven jogged my elbow." On which Seven looked up and said "That's right, Five! Always lay the blame on others!" *"You'd* better not talk!" said Five. "I heard the Queen say only yesterday you deserved to be beheaded." "What for?" said the one who had spoken first. "That's none of *your* business, Two!" said Seven. "Yes, it *is* his business!" said Five.'

Ralph Steadman. Dennis Dobson, London, 1967.

'The three soldiers wandered about for a minute or two, looking for them, and then quietly marched off after the others.'

J.P.M. Alice's Wonderland Birthday Book, Griffith & Farran, London, 1884.

' "You sha'n't be beheaded!" said Alice, and she put them into a large flower-pot that stood near.'

W.M. Walker. John Lane, The Bodley Head Ltd., London, 1907.

'She was looking about for some way of escape, and wondering whether she could get away without being seen, when she noticed a curious appearance in the air: it puzzled her very much at first, but after watching it for a minute or two she made it out to be a grin, and she said to herself "It's the Cheshire-Cat: now I shall have somebody to talk to."

Graham Ovenden, oil, 1970.

50

Lewis Carroll, 1886.

A.L. Bowley, 1921.

Robert Högfeldt, 1945.

Charles Robinson, 1907.

Willy Pogany, 1929.

The Mad Hatter's Tea Party

Blanche McManus. A. Wessels, New York, 1900. (opposite)

Max Ernst. *Lewis Carroll's Wunderhorn,* Manus Press, Stuttgart, 1970. (overleaf)

'The chief difficulty Alice found at first was in managing her flamingo; she succeeded in getting its body tucked away, comfortably enough, under her arm, with its legs hanging down, but generally, just as she had got its neck nicely straightened out, and was going to give the hedgehog a blow with its head, it *would* twist itself round and look up in her face.'

Fritz Haaken, George Bitter Verlag, Berlin, 1968.

55

Chapter 9

THE MOCK TURTLE'S STORY

'The Gryphon sat up and rubbed its eyes; then it watched the Queen until she was out of sight: then it chuckled. "What fun!" said the Gryphon, half to itself, half to Alice.'

Charles Robinson. Cassell & Co. Ltd., London, 1907.

'They had not gone far before they saw the Mock Turtle in the distance, sitting sad and lonely on a little ledge of rock, and, as they came nearer, Alice could hear him sighing as if his heart would break. She pitied him deeply. "What is his sorrow?" she asked the Gryphon. And the Gryphon answered, very nearly in the same words as before, "It's all his fancy, that; he hasn't got no sorrow, you know. Come on!" '

Robert Högfeldt. Jan Forlag, Stockholm, 1945.

' "You can't think how glad I am to see you again, you dear old thing!" said the Duchess, as she tucked her arm affectionately into Alice's, and they walked off together.'

Thomas Heath Robinson. William Collins, London, 1922.

Chapter 10
THE LOBSTER QUADRILLE

'So they began solemnly dancing round and round Alice, every now and then treading on her toes when they passed too close, and waving their fore-paws to mark the time.'

Sir John Tenniel. Macmillan, London, 1866

' "What trial is it?" Alice panted as she ran; but the Gryphon answered "Come on and ran the faster." '

Willy Pogany. E.P. Dutton & Co., New York, 1929.

' "Come on!" cried the Gryphon, and, taking Alice by the hand, it hurried off, without waiting for the end of the song.'

Millicent Sowerby. Chatto & Windus, London, 1907.

Chapter 11

WHO STOLE THE TARTS?

'The King and Queen of Hearts were seated on their throne....the Knave was standing before them, in chains with a soldier on each side'

Harry Furniss. *The World's Great Books in Outline,* Hammerton, London, 1926.

‘ "The Queen of Hearts, she made some tarts,
All on a summer day:
The Knave of Hearts, he stole those tarts
And took them quite away!" ’

Gwynedd Hudson. Hodder & Stoughton, London, 1922.

‘ "Stupid things!" Alice began in a loud indignant voice; but she stopped herself hastily, for the White Rabbit cried out "Silence in the court!", and the King put on his spectacles and looked anxiously round, to make out who was talking.'

Graham Ovenden, oil, 1970.

'Alice had never been in a court of justice before, but she had read about them in books, and she was quite pleased to find that she knew the name of nearly everything there.'

Thomas Maybank. G. Routledge & Sons Ltd., London, 1907.

'The next witness was the Duchess's cook. She carried the pepper-box in her hand, and Alice guessed who it was, even before she got into the court, by the way the people near the door began sneezing all at once.'

K.M.R. S.W. Partridge & Co., London, 1908.

'Here the Queen put on her spectacles, and began staring hard at the Hatter, who turned pale and fidgeted. "Give your evidence," said the King; "and don't be nervous, or I'll have you executed on the spot.'

Harry Furniss. *The World's Great Books in Outline*, Hammerton, London, 1926.

' "You may go," said the King, and the Hatter hurriedly left the court, without even waiting to put his shoes on.'

Charles Robinson. Cassell & Co., London, 1907.

Chapter 12

Alice's Evidence

' "They told me you had been to her,
 And mentioned me to him:
She gave me a good character,
 But said I could not swim.

He sent them word I had not gone
 (We know it to be true):
If she should push the matter on,
 What would become of you?

I gave her one, they gave him two,
 You gave us three or more;
They all returned from him to you,
 Though they were mine before.

If I or she should chance to be
 Involved in this affair,
He trusts to you to set them free,
 Exactly as we were." '

' "Here!" cried Alice, quite forgetting in the flurry of the moment how large she had grown in the last few minutes, and she jumped up in such a hurry that she tipped over the jury-box with the edge of her skirt, upsetting all the jury men on to the heads of the crowd below, and there they lay sprawling about, reminding her very much of a globe of gold fish she had accidentally spilt the week before.'

A.E. Jackson.   Henry Frowde: Hodder & Stoughton, London, 1915.

66

'Alice looked at the jury-box, and saw that, in her haste, she had put the Lizard in head downwards, and the poor little thing was waving its tail about in a melancholy way, being quite unable to move. She soon got it out again, and put it right; "not that it signifies much," she said to herself; "I should think it would be *quite* as much use in the trial one way up as the other.'

Sir John Tenniel, Macmillan, London, 1866.

' "Oh, I've had such a curious dream!" said Alice. And she told her sister, as well as she could remember them, all these strange adventures of hers'

W.M. Walker. John Lane, The Bodley Head, 1907.

Through the Looking-glass
and
What Alice Found There

'Twas brillig, and the slithy toves
  Did gyre and gimble in the wabe:
All mimsy were the borogoves,
  And the mome raths outgrabe.

"Beware the Jabberwock, my son!
  The jaws that bite, the claws that catch!
Beware the Jubjub bird, and shun
  The frumious Bandersnatch!"

He took his vorpal sword in hand:
  Long time the manxome foe he sought -
So rested he by the Tumtum tree,
  And stood awhile in thought.

And, as in uffish thought he stood,
  The Jabberwock, with eyes of flame,
Came whiffing through the tulgey wood,
  And burbled as it came!

One, two! One, two! And through and through
  The vorpal blade went snicker-snack!
He left it dead, and with its head
  He went galumphing back.

"And hast thou slain the Jabberwock?
  Come to my arms, my beamish boy!
O frabjous day! Callooh! Callay!"
  He chortled in his joy.

'Twas brillig, and the slithy toves
  Did gyre and gimble in the wabe:
All mimsy were the borogoves,
  And the mome raths outgrabe.

One, two! One, two! And through and
    through
  The vorpal blade went snicker-snack!
He left it dead, and with its head
  He went galumphing back.

Maraja. W.H. Allen, London. 1959.

Gwynedd Hudson. Hodder & Stoughton, London, 1922.

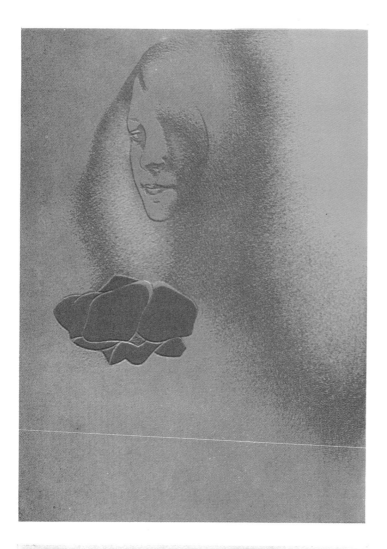

"For instance, now, there's the King's messenger. He's in prison now, being punished! and the trial doesn't even begin till next Wednesday: and of course the crime comes last of all." Peter Blake 1970.

(*top left*) **Graham Ovenden** Screenprint 24·4 × 18·1 cm, 1970.
". . . and Alice looked round eager to see the Queen."

(*left*) **Peter Blake** Watercolour for screenprint 24·4 × 18·1 cm, 1970.
"For instance, now, there's the King's messenger. He's in prison now, being punished! and the trial doesn't even begin till next Wednesday: and of course the crime comes last of all."

(*above*) **Willy Pogany** Book illustration, 1929.
"I ca'n't help it," said Alice very meekly; "I'm growing". *Alice's Adventures in Wonderland*, E. P. Dutton & Co., New York, 1929.

THROUGH THE LOOKING-GLASS

AND WHAT ALICE FOUND THERE

by

LEWIS CARROLL

Title page, **Robert Murray.**   Illustrations by Peter Newell, Harper, New York, 1902

Chapter 1

Looking-glass House

'The King immediately fell flat on his back, and lay perfectly still; and Alice was a little alarmed at what she had done, and went round the room to see if she could find any water to throw over him. However, she could find nothing but a bottle of ink, and when she got back with it she found he had recovered, and he and the Queen were talking together in a frightened whisper.'

J. Morton Sale. William Clowes, London, 1933.

'So Alice picked him up very gently, and lifted him across more slowly than she had lifted the Queen, that she mightn't take his breath away: but before she put him on the table, she thought she might as well dust him a little, he was so covered with ashes.'

Peter Blake, screenprint, 1970.

Chapter 2

THE GARDEN OF LIVE FLOWERS

'She had not been walking a minute before she found herself face to face with the Red Queen, and full in sight of the hill she had been so long aiming at.'

Franklin Hughes. Cheshire House, New York, 1931.

' "Where do you come from?" said the Red Queen. "And where are you going? Look up, speak nicely, and don't twiddle your fingers all the time." Alice attended to all these instructions, and explained, as well as she could, that she had lost her way.'

Peter Newell. Harper Bros., New York, 1902.

Chapter 3

Looking-glass Insects

'this was anything but a regular bee: in fact, it was an elephant — as Alice soon found out, though the idea quite took her breath away at first. "And what enormous flowers they must be!" was her next idea. "Something like cottages with the roofs taken off, and stalks put to them — " '

Robert Högfeldt. Jan Forlag, Stockholm, 1945.

'All this time the Guard was looking at her, first through a telescope, then through a microscope, and then through an opera-glass. At last he said "You're travelling the wrong way," and shut up the window, and went away.'

Sir John Tenniel. Macmillan, 1872.

The Bread-and-butter-fly.

The Rocking-horse-fly.

The Snap-dragon-fly.

Chapter 4

Tweedledum and Tweedledee

Philip Gough. The Heirloom Press, c. 1940.

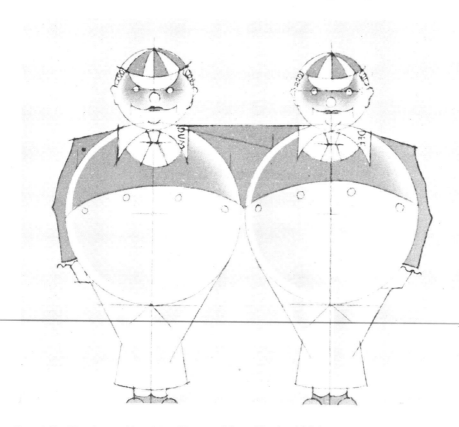

Franklin Hughes. Cheshire House, New York, 1931.

'They were standing under a tree, each with an arm round the other's neck, and Alice knew which was which in a moment, because one of them had 'DUM' embroidered on his collar, and the other 'DEE'. "I suppose they've each got 'TWEEDLE' round at the back of the collar," she said to herself.'

Peter Blake, screenprint, 1970.

' "O Oysters," said the Carpenter,
    "You've had a pleasant run!
  Shall we be trotting home again?"
    But answer came there none -
  And this was scarcely odd, because
    They'd eaten every one." '

Sir John Tenniel. Macmillan, 1872.

' " The sun was shining on the sea,
    Shining with all his might:
  He did his very best to make
    The billows smooth and bright-
  And this was odd, because it was
    The middle of the night.

The moon was shining sulkily,
    Because she thought the sun
  Had got no business to be there
    After the day was done-
  'It's very rude of him,' she said,
    'To come and spoil the fun!'" '

Maraja.   W.H. Allen, London, 1959

'But four young Oysters hurried up,
All eager for the treat:
Their coats were brushed, their faces washed,
Their shoes were clean and neat —
And this was odd, because, you know,
They hadn't any feet.'

Blanche McManus. A. Wessels & Co., New York, 1900

Chapter 5

WOOL AND WATER

' "I wish *I* could manage to be glad!" the Queen said. "Only I never can remember the rule. You must be very happy, living in this wood, and being glad whenever you like!" '

J. Morton Sale, William Clowes, London, 1933.

'suddenly the needles turned into oars in her hands, and she found they were in a little boat, gliding along between banks: so there was nothing for it but to do her best.'

Mervyn Peake. Allen Wingate, London, 1954.

Chapter 6

HUMPTY DUMPTY

'The egg only got larger and larger and more and more human: when she had come within a few yards of it, she saw that it had eyes and a nose and a mouth; and when she had come close to it, she saw clearly that it was HUMPTY DUMPTY himself.'

Philip Gough. The Heirloom Press, c. 1940.

'Humpty Dumpty was sitting, with his legs crossed like a Turk, on the top of a high wall - such a narrow one Alice quite wondered how he could keep his balance - and, as his eyes were steadily fixed in the opposite direction, and he didn't take the least notice of her, she thought he must be a stuffed figure, after all.'

E.B. Thurstan. Juvenile Productions Ltd., London, c. 1930.

Chapter 7

THE LION AND THE UNICORN

'The King was evidently very uncomfortable at having to sit down between the two great creatures; but there was no other place for him.'

Robert Högfeldt. Jan Forlag, Stockholm, 1945.

'But before Alice could answer him, the drums began. Where the noise came from, she couldn't make out; the air seemed full of it, and it rang through and through her head till she felt quite deafened.'

Sir John Tenniel. Macmillan, 1872.

'Hatta looked round and nodded, and went on with his bread-and-butter. "Were you happy in prison, dear child?" said Haigha. Hatta looked round once more, and this time a tear or two trickled down his cheek; but not a word would he say. "Speak, can't you!" Haigha cried impatiently. But Hatta only munched away, and drank some more tea.'

Mervyn Peake. Allen Wingate, London, 1954.

Chapter 8

"It's My Own Invention"

'they began banging away at each other with such fury that Alice got behind a tree to be out of the way of the blows.'

Blanche McManus, A.Wessels, New York, 1900.

'The Knight looked so solemn about it that Alice did not dare to laugh.'

J. Morton Sale. William Clowes, London, 1933.

90

' "Thank you very much," said Alice. "May I help you off with your helmet?"
It was evidently more than he could manage by himself: however she managed to
shake him out of it at last!'

E.B. Thurstan. Juvenile Productions Ltd., London, c. 1930.

Chapter 9

Queen Alice

Mervyn Peake. Allen Wingate, London, 1954.

Robert Högfeldt. Jan Forlag, Stockholm, 1945.

' "What am I to do?" exclaimed Alice, looking about in great perplexity, as first one round head and then the other rolled down from her shoulder, and lay like a heavy lump in her lap.'

Peter Blake, screenprint, 1970.

"Well, this is grand!" said Alice." I never expected I should be a Queen so soon.

'The leg of mutton got up in the dish and made a little bow to Alice: and Alice returned the bow, not knowing whether to be frightened or amused.'

Peter Newell. Harper Bros., New York, 1902.

94

'Alice knocked and rang in vain for a long time, but at last a very old Frog, who was sitting under a tree, got up and hobbled slowly towards her; he was dressed in bright yellow, and had enormous boots on.'

Sir John Tenniel, Macmillan, London, 1872.

Chapter 10

Shaking

'She took her off the table as she spoke and shook her backwards and forwards with all her might.'

E.B. Thurstan. Juvenile Productions, London c.1930

Chapter 11

Waking

'it really was a kitten, after all.'

Sir John Tenniel. Macmillan, London, 1872.

96

Chapter 12

Which Dreamed It?

Maria Barrera, Editorial Bruguera, S.A., Barcelona, 1956.

' "Let's pretend the glass has got all soft like gauze, so we can get through. Why, it's turning into a sort of mist now, I declare! It'll be easy enough to get through - " '.

'In another moment Alice was through the glass, and had jumped down lightly into the Looking-glass room'.

Sir John Tenniel, Macmillan, London 1872.

BIBLIOGRAPHY OF ILLUSTRATED
ENGLISH LANGUAGE EDITIONS

ALICE IN WONDERLAND

ADAMS, Frank. Oxford University Press, London, 1912.
ACCORNERO, V. Murray's Sales & Service, London, 1968.
ACKROYD, Winifred. London, 1930.
ALLEN, Olive. Edward Arnold, London, 1910.
APPLETON, Honor C. Harrap, London and New York, 1936.
ATTWELL, Mabel Lucie. Raphael Tuck, London and New York, 1910.

BACKHOUSE, G.W. William Collins, London, 1951.
BLUM, Alexa. Gilberton, New York, 1948.
BOWLEY, Ada. McKay, Philadelphia,1926.
BOWLEY, A.L. Raphael Tuck, London, 1921.
BROCK, E.M. U.K., undated.
BRUCE, Suzanne. Rand, McNally, Chicago, 1951.
CARROLL, Lewis, *Alice's Adventures Under Ground,* Macmillan, London, 1886. New York, 1932.
CHAMBERS with GORDON and SPENCER. U.S.A., 1951.
CLOKE, Rene. P.R. Gawthorne, London, 1944.
COONEY, F.C. Rand, Chicago, 1929.
COOPER, John with David WALSH. Ward Lock, 1962.
CORY, F.Y. Rand, Chicago, 1902.
DALI, Salvador. Random House, New York, 1969.
DEMPSTER, Al. Simon & Schuster, New York, 1951.
DISNEY, Walt. Disney Productions, California, 1948.
DYER, Gil. Foulsham, London, 1934.
LeFANU, Brinsley. Stead, London, 1907.
FEDERER, A.C. with A.E. JACKSON, U.S.A., 1930.
FOLKARD, Charles. A. & C. Black, London, 1929.
FURNISS, Harry. *The World's Great Books in Outline,* Hammerton, London, 1926.
GEE, Hugh. Adprint, London, 1948.
GOODALL, A.S. Blackie, London, 1965.
GREENE, Julia with Helen PETTES. Cupples, New York, 1917.
GUTMANN, see PEASE.
HALL, Douglas. L. Miller, London, 1960.
HAWES, Walter. W. Scott, London, 1908.
HENDERSON, Hume. Reader's Library, London, 1932.
HERFORD, O. Ginn, Boston, 1917.
HIDALGO, Rylee, London, undated.
HONEYBOURNE, Rosemary. McClelland & Stewart, Toronto, 1969.
HUEHNERGARTH, John. Winstons, New York, 1952.
HUDSON, Gwynedd M.. Hodder & Stoughton, London, Dudd, New York, 1922.
JACKSON, A.E. Henry Frowde:Hodder & Stoughton, New York, 1914, London, 1915.
JARRETT, Douglas. Reader's Library, London, 1928.
JOHNSTONE, Janet with Anne GRAHAM. World Distributors, London, 1968.
KAY, Gertrude. A. Lippincott, Philadelphia, 1923.
KIRK, M.L. Stokes, New York, 1904.

L'ALPINO. Odhams, London, 1966.
LAURENCIN, Marie. Black Sun Press, Paris, 1930.
LEONE, Sergio. Golden Pleasure Books, London, 1962, New York, 1963.
LIBRAGHI and AQUENZA. Odhams, London, 1963.
McEUNE, R.E. Milner, London, 1908.
McKEAN, Emma. McLoughlin,, Massachusetts, 1943.
McMANUS, Blanche. Mansfield, New York, 1896, Ward Lock, London, 1907.
MATULAY, Laszlo. Grosset & Dunlap, New York, 1951.
MARAJA, Grosset & Dunlap. New York, 1957. W. H. Allen, London, 1958.
MAYBANK, Thomas. Routledge, London, 1907.
MONRO, Helen. *World's Treasury of Great Stories,* Daily Express, London, 1933. Nelson, London, 1936.
NASH, A.A. U.K., undated.
NEWELL, Peter. Harper, New York, 1901.
NEWSOME. Warne, London, undated.
NORFIELD, Edgar. William Collins, London, undated.
OVENDEN, Graham. Not yet published.
OVERNELL, Emily. Everett, London, 1912.
PEARS, Charles with T. H. ROBINSON. William Collins, London, 1922.
PEASE GUTMANN, Bessie. Dodge, New York, 1907. Milne, London, 1908.
PETTES, Helen. Cupples, New York, 1917.
POGANY, Willy. E.P.Dutton, New York, 1929.
R.K.M. S.W.Partridge, London, 1908.
RACKHAM, Arthur. William Heinemann, London, 1907. Garden City, New York, 1907.
RADO, A. W.H. Cornelius, London, 1954.
READER, E.K. Philips & Tacey, London, undated.
RICHARDSON, Nelson. London, 1920.
RILEY, Harry. Arthur Barron, London, 1945.
ROBINSON, Charles. Cassell, London and New York, 1907.
ROBINSON, Normy. Children's Press, London, 1963.
ROBINSON, T.H. William Collins, London, 1922.
ROSS, Alice. Nimmo, Edinburgh, 1907.
ROUNTREE, Harry. Nelson, London, 1908. The Children's Press, London, undated.
SCHERMELE, Willy. Juvenile Productions, London, undated.
SEXTON, D.R. J. F. Shaw, London, 1937. Juvenile Productions, London, 1933.
SINCLAIR, J.R. Sunday School Union, London, 1909.
SMITH, Jessie. U.S.A., undated.
SOPER, Eileen. Harrap, London, 1947.
SOPER, George. Headley, London, 1911. Baker, New York, 1911.
SOWERBY, Millicent. Chatto & Windus, London, 1907. Duffield, New York, 1908.

STANLEY, Diana. U.K., 1954.
STEADMAN, Ralph. Dobson, London, 1967.
TARRANT, Margaret. Ward Lock, London, 1916.
TENNIEL, Sir John. Macmillan, London, 1865.
Appleton, New York, 1866.
THOMSON, E. Gertrude. *The Nursery Alice,*
Macmillan, London, 1899. New York, 1890.
TORREY, Marjorie. Random House, New York,
1955. Purnell, London, 1946.

TOVEY, R.M. William Collins, London, 1938.
WALKER, W.H. John Lane, The Bodley Head,
London and New York, 1907.
WALSH, David. Blackie, London, 1954.
WOODWARD, Alice. Bell, London and New
York, 1913.

THROUGH THE LOOKING-GLASS

BRIDGEMAN, F. and others. Cromwell, New
York, 1900.
BLAKE, Peter. Not yet published.
CLOKE, Rene. P.R. Gawthorne, London, 1950.
COLLINSON, Marjorie. Maxton, New York, 1947.
CORY, F. Rand, Chicago, 1917.
FULLERTON, Nan. U.K., undated.
HUGHES, Franklin. Cheshire House, New York, 1931.
KAY, Gertrude. Lippincott, Philadelphia, 1929.
KIRK, M.L. Stokes, New York, 1905.
KREDEL, Fritz. Random House, New York, 1946.
LEONARD. Golden Pleasure Books, London, 1962.

McMANUS, Blanche. Mansfield, New York, 1899.
MARAJA. W.H.Allen, London, 1958.
MONRO, H. Nelson, London,.1953.
NEWELL, Peter. Harper, New York, 1902.
PEASE GUTMANN, Bessie. Dodge, New York, 1909.
PRITTIE, Edwin. Philadelphia, 1929.
ROUNTREE, Harry. U.K., 1928.
STEADMAN, Ralph. McGibbon & Kee. NYP.
TENNIEL, Sir John. Macmillan, London, 1871.
New York, 1872.
THURSTAN, Edgar B. Juvenile Productions,
London, undated.

ALICE IN WONDERLAND AND THROUGH THE LOOKING-GLASS

ABBOTT, Eleonore. Philadelphia, 1912.
ADOHERTY, Dorothy. U.K., undated.
BAYNES, Pauline. U.K., 1950.
BLITHE. Studley Press, London, undated.
BRYAN, B. U.S.A., 1969.
CARD, Linda. Racine, Wisconsin, 1945.
CLEMENTS, M.L. Hutchinson, London, 1934.
COLLES, Dorothy. William Collins, London, 1954.
COLLINSON, Marjorie. Maxton, New York, 1947.
COOK, Donald. U.S.A., 1961.
DAVIS. U.S.A., 1910.
GOUGH, Philip. The Heirloom Press, London,
undated.
HOGFELDT, Robert. Jan Forlag, Stockholm, 1945.
KREDEL, Fritz. U.S.A., undated.
LEONARD. Golden Pleasure Books, London, 1962.
MACKNIGHT, Ninon. Platt & Munk, New York,
1937.
McMANUS, Blanche. A. Wessels, New York, 1900.

MONRO, Helen. London, undated.
MORRIS, Patricia. Beaverbrook Newspapers, London,
undated.
MOUNTFORT, Irene. William Collins, London, 1939.
PAFLIN, Roberta. Whitman, New York, 1955.
PEAKE, Mervyn. Allen Wingate, London, 1954.
PRITTIE, Edwin. Winston, Philadelphia, 1923.
ROUNTREE, Harry. William Collins, London, 1928.
SALE, J. Morton. William Clowes, London, 1933.
SCHROEDER, T. U.S.A., 1970.
STEVENS, Beatrice. Collier, New York, 1903.
TENNIEL, Sir John. Macmillan, London, 1887.
New York, 1881.
THURSTAN, Edgar. Odhams, London, undated.
VAN HOFSTEN, Hugo. U.S.A., undated.
WATSON, A.H. William Collins, London, 1937.
WELLING, Gertrude. Seers, New York, 1926.
WIESGARD, Leonard. Harper, New York, 1949.
WINTER, Milo. Rand, Chicago, 1916.

SELECTED BIBLIOGRAPHY OF WORKS ON CARROLL

Bowman, Isa. *The Story of Lewis Carroll.* J.M. Dent, 1899.

Burdick, Loraine. *Alice in Wonderland.* Celebrity Doll Club Magazine, February, 1970.

Collingwood, Stuart Dodgson. *The Life and Letters of Lewis Carroll.* T. Fisher Unwin, 1898. *The Lewis Carroll Picture Book.* T. Fisher Unwin, 1899.

Doyle, Brian. *The Who's Who of Children's Literature.* Hugh Evelyn, London, 1968.

Gilmore, Maeve. *A World Away. A Memoir of Mervyn Peake.* Gollancz, 1970.

Green, R.L. *The Story of Lewis Carroll.* Methuen, 1949. *The Diaries of Lewis Carroll.* Cassell, 1953.

Hudson, Derek. *Lewis Carroll.* Constable, 1954.

Lennon, Florence Becker. *Victoria Through the Looking-Glass.* Simon & Schuster, New York, 1945.

Madan, Falconer (ed). *Lewis Carroll Centenary Exhibition.* J. & E. Bumpus, 1932.

de la Mare, Walter. *Lewis Carroll.* Faber & Faber, 1932.

Mespoulet, Marguerite. *Creators of Wonderland.* Arrow Editions, 1934.

Reed, Langford. *The Life of Lewis Carroll.* W. & G. Foyle, 1932.

Smith, R.D. Hilton. *Alice One Hundred.* Adelphi Book Shop, 1966.

Taylor, A.L. *The White Knight.* Oliver & Boyd.

Weaver, Warren. *Alice in Many Tongues.* University of Wisconsin Press, 1964.

Williams, S.H. *A Bibliography of the Writings of Lewis Carroll.* The Bookman's Journal, 1924.

Williams & Madan. *A Handbook of the Literature of the Rev. C.L. Dodgson.* Oxford University Press, 1931.

Williams & Madan revised by R.L. Green. *The Lewis Carroll Handbook.* Oxford University Press, 1962.

Wood, J.P. *The Snark was a Boojum.* Pantheon Books, 1966.

Catalogue of an Exhibition at Colombia University. Colombia University Press, 1932.

Mary Hilton Badcock, the model for Tenniel's Alice.

741.64
O   Ovenden
              Illustrators of Alice in
         Wonderland and Through the
         looking glass
                   Date Due
